BASEBALL
IN ROCHESTER

6/03

MOST LIKELY TO SUCCEED. The most famous alumnus of the Rochester Red Wings is Cal Ripken Jr., who is pictured here before a 1981 game at old Silver Stadium. Before starting his legendary big-league career with the Baltimore Orioles, Ripken spent his final minor-league season with the Wings, earning International League Rookie of the Year honors. (Courtesy of Hour Glass Antiques.)

BASEBALL
IN ROCHESTER

Scott Pitoniak

ARCADIA

ISBN 0-7385-1169-2

First printed in 2003.

Published by Arcadia Publishing,
an imprint of Tempus Publishing Inc.
2A Cumberland Street
Charleston, SC 29401

Printed in Great Britain.

Library of Congress Catalog Card Number: 2002116453

For all general information, contact Arcadia Publishing:
Telephone 843-853-2070
Fax 843-853-0044
E-mail sales@arcadiapublishing.com

For customer service and orders:
Toll-free 1-888-313-2665

Visit us on the Internet at www.arcadiapublishing.com.

SILVER STADIUM. For 68 years, Silver Stadium, at 500 Norton Street on Rochester's north side, was home to Rochester Red Wings baseball.

CONTENTS

ACKNOWLEDGMENTS

Baseball is a team game. Book publishing is, too. So, I would like to doff my cap to the many teammates who helped me pull this off.

My thanks go to an All-Star lineup that includes Tiffany Howe, Amy Sutton, and Will Willoughby at Arcadia Publishing; Tom Flynn and Dave Hunke at the Rochester *Democrat and Chronicle* for their permission to reprint scores of photographs from our newspaper's files; Matt Cipro, Chuck Hinkel, Gary Larder, Dan Mason, Will Rumbold, Nick Sciarratta, and Naomi Silver of the Rochester Red Wings; rabid Red Wing fans Pete Dobrovitz, Dan Guilfoyle, and Gary Siwicki; Lea Kemp and Gian Carlo Cervone at the Rochester Museum and Science Center; W.C. Burdick and the National Baseball Hall of Fame Library staff; Rochester city historian Ruth Rosenberg-Naparsteck and local baseball historian Priscilla Astifan; Tony Wells for the photographs from the Hickok Belt dinners; John Ignizio; Roxie Sinkler; Mark Rucker of Transcendental Graphics; and Jamie Germano, Kevin Higley, Barbara Jean Germano, and all the other talented photographers who have provided us with the lasting images of baseball in Rochester.

Lastly, and most importantly, I would like to thank the heart of my order: my late parents, Andrew and Edna Pitoniak; my wife, Susan; and our children, Amy and Christopher. Their love and support through the years has been priceless.

MR. ROCHESTER BASEBALL. Through the years, Joe Altobelli has done everything for the Rochester Red Wings but sell peanuts and Cracker Jack. He has been a player, coach, manager, general manager, and color commentator on radio broadcasts of Wings games. Altobelli was the winningest manager during the Baltimore Orioles affiliation, guiding Rochester to Governors' Cup titles in 1971 and 1974. Even after managing the Orioles to their last World Series title in 1983, he continued to make Rochester his off-season home.

INTRODUCTION
A GAME ROOTED IN ROCHESTER

You will not find any "Birthplace of Baseball" signs in Rochester, but if Stephen Fox had his way, you would. The author of a 1995 book that debunks long-held sports myths, Fox contends that baseball's origins can be traced to Rochester, not Cooperstown. His book, titled *Big Leagues*, refers to newspaper accounts of baseball being played regularly during the summer of 1825 at Mumford's Meadow near the Genesee River, where downtown Rochester now stands.

Although Fox's revelation did not result in a clamoring for the relocation of the National Baseball Hall of Fame and Museum, it did remind people that Rochester's baseball roots run almost as deep as the gorges at nearby Letchworth State Park, the Grand Canyon of the East.

Since the economic boom times of the early 19th century, baseball has been inextricably interwoven into the fabric of the Rochester community. Decades before George Eastman (the city's most famous entrepreneur and philanthropist) brought photography to the masses, the game was being played in the Flower City.

You would be hard-pressed to find a city with a longer and richer minor-league baseball tradition. Rochester fielded its first all-professional team in 1877, and since that time, the oldest member of the International League has won a record 19 pennants.

Nineteen members of the Baseball Hall of Fame have Rochester connections, and that number will increase by two in the not-so-distant future when former Red Wing players Cal Ripken Jr. and Eddie Murray are inducted. Not surprisingly, Ripken's propensity for streaking took flight as a Wing during the 1981 season. Baseball's iron man did not miss a start in Rochester, his final minor-league stop before big-league stardom.

Rochester was also the place where Stan "Then a Young Man" Musial honed his skills before embarking on his legendary major-league career during the summer of 1941.

The gospel according to Luke was preached at Red Wing Stadium in the early 1960s by Luke Easter, a mountainous slugger who warmed fans with his kindness and awed them with his light-tower-topping home runs and gusty strikeouts.

Rochester, too, was where former Red Wings utility infielder Ron Shelton gathered ground balls and material for *Bull Durham*, his Academy Award–nominated comedy about life in the bush leagues.

Among those who pitched for Rochester was Daniel Boone—not the famous frontiersman, but rather his seventh-generation nephew whose dancing knuckleball resulted in a no-hitter for the Wings in a July 23, 1990 game.

"Slingin' Sammy" Baugh, one of the National Football League's all-time best quarterbacks, once wore the Rochester flannels. His .183 batting average in 1938 undoubtedly convinced him he would have better success hitting receivers than curve balls.

The most versatile performer in Rochester baseball history has to be Joe Altobelli. The man who managed the Baltimore Orioles to their last World Series championship 20 years ago has been a player, coach, manager, general manager, and radio color man for the Wings. Entering his 53rd season in professional baseball, Altobelli said he would like to mow the outfield grass at Frontier Field and add "groundskeeper" to his resume. Rochesterians fondly refer to him as "Mr. Baseball." The same title was once bestowed on Morrie Silver. Although he never suited up, the former Red Wings president recorded the biggest save in team history when he initiated a community stock drive in the mid-1950s to keep professional baseball in town.

Rochester baseball has often been about going the distance—long distance. In a 1950 game against Jersey City, Wings starter Tom Poholsky pitched 22 innings to out-duel Andy Tomasic for a 3-2 victory at old Red Wing Stadium. For sheer length, however, nothing can match the 1981 contest between the Wings and the Pawtucket Red Sox. That 33-inning marathon, won by the PawSox, remains the longest game in the 134-year history of professional baseball. The game actually started in mid-April and concluded 65 days later. Stars for Rochester included Dave Huppert, who caught 31 innings, and Jim Umbarger, who gave new meaning to the term "long-reliever" with 10 shutout innings.

They say birds of a feather flock together, and that has been true of Rochester and its parent clubs. From 1928 to 1960, the Wings were affiliated with the St. Louis Cardinals, and from 1961 until the fall of 2002, when they signed on with the Minnesota Twins, they were the top farm club of the Orioles. Along the way, the Wings have won 10 Governors' Cup titles. Manager Billy Southworth's 1930 club, which boasted seven .300 hitters in the starting lineup, and Altobelli's 1971 team, led by Bobby Grich and Don Baylor, are regarded among the best in minor-league history.

These stars, and more, are captured in the more than 180 photographs in *Baseball in Rochester*. The images will give you a sense of the sport's rich history in western New York and will help you understand why *Baseball America* magazine named Rochester "Baseball City, U.S.A."

—Scott Pitoniak

One
THE EARLY YEARS

AND A ONE, AND A TWO. This 1860 cover illustration from a polka dedicated to one of Rochester's first organized teams is believed to be the earliest known baseball lithograph. J.H. Kalbfleisch composed the polka, which was played after Live Oak Baseball Club games. Joseph P. Shaw designed the lithograph.

AN EXERCISE IN BASEBALL. Two teams, one white and one black, play a baseball game during recess at Rochester's old Western House of Refuge, a boys reformatory school. The photograph was taken by F.W. Bacon c. 1875. (Courtesy of Mark Rucker, Transcendental Graphics.)

MUSTACHE MASHERS. The 1884 Rochesters were one of the city's most successful clubs of the 19th century. This photograph was taken after the Billy Burke–managed team thrashed the Hudsons 17-1 for the city championship.

THE OLD HOMESTEAD. Culver Field was home to Rochester's professional baseball teams from 1898 to 1907. The first Culver Field was destroyed by fire in 1892.

MAJORING IN BASEBALL. Rochester's only major-league team, the Hop Bitters, played in the American Association during the summer of 1890. This engraving of that club appeared on the cover of the *Sporting Life,* the 19th-century equivalent of *Sports Illustrated.* Thanks to the pitching of "Big Bob" Barr, Rochester resided in second place for the first several weeks of the season. However, the good times did not last. Rochester finished in fifth place with a 63-63 record and, the following summer, returned to the minor leagues.

FIRST CHAMPIONS. Manager Al Buckenberger's feisty Bronchos posted a 73-44 record to win the 1899 Eastern League title and bring home Rochester's first professional championship. Buck's Bronchos were as well known for their intimidating tactics as they were for their baseball skills. Opponents claimed that first baseman Harry O'Hagan placed a hatpin in his glove with just enough of the point protruding to "vaccinate" runners as they dived back into first on pick-off attempts. Despite numerous complaints and inspections, umpires were unable to find a pin in O'Hagan's mitt.

The Start of a Three-Peat. Managed by former major-leaguer "Big Jawn" Ganzel, the Hustlers won the 1909 pennant, the first of three consecutive championships by Rochester.

In the Cards. Six members of the Rochester Hustlers were featured in the T-206 tobacco card series.

LINING UP. The Rochester Hustlers take the field at Baseball Park on Bay Street before the opening game of the 1912 season. Mayor Hiram Edgerton stands to the right. The Hustlers won the game with Providence 2-1. (Courtesy of the Albert R. Stone Negative Collection, Rochester Museum and Science Center.)

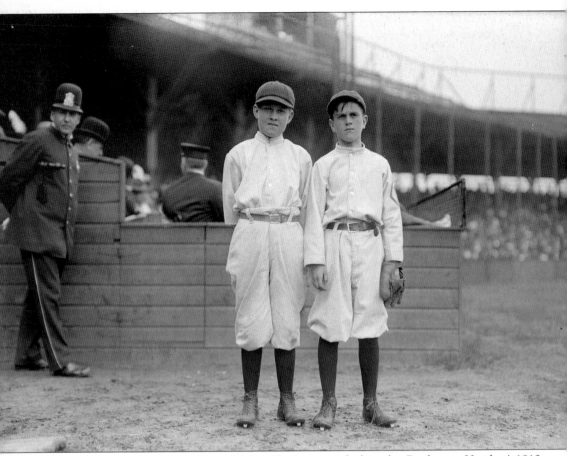

Bat Boys. Joseph Neff (left) and John Sharkey pose before the Rochester Hustlers' 1912 season opener at Baseball Park. (Courtesy of the Albert R. Stone Negative Collection, Rochester Museum and Science Center.)

MANAGING JUST FINE. Rochester Hustlers manager John Ganzel (in uniform) is shown standing alongside a Hudson 6 automobile, a gift from Rochester fans in appreciation for Ganzel's deeds. To the right of Ganzel is Mayor Hiram Edgerton, who is making the presentation before the 1913 season opener at Baseball Park. To the far right are Charles Owen and team owner Charlie Chapin (arms crossed). (Courtesy of the Albert R. Stone Negative Collection, Rochester Museum and Science Center.)

SARTORIAL SPLENDOR. Thousands of well-dressed fans fill the bleachers at Baseball Park for Rochester's May 15, 1909 opener. It was common for fans of that era to dress up for games. (Courtesy of the Albert R. Stone Negative Collection, Rochester Museum and Science Center.)

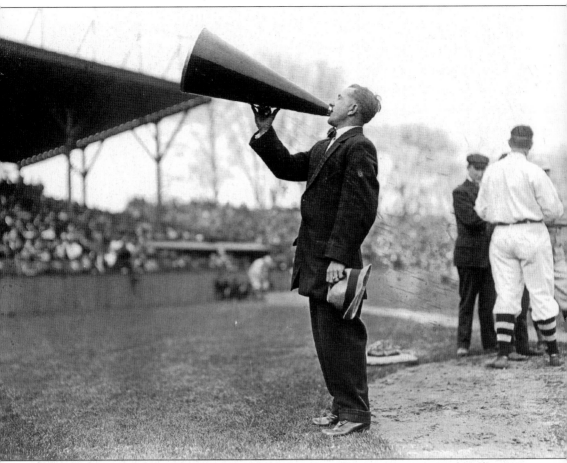

"LADIES AND GENTLEMEN." Bobby Dorr is using a large megaphone to announce the pitcher and catcher for the opening game of the 1912 season at Baseball Park. These were the days before public address systems. (Courtesy of the Albert R. Stone Negative Collection, Rochester Museum and Science Center.)

FULL HOUSE. This photograph offers a panoramic view of the 13,000 spectators who stuffed Baseball Park for Rochester's Eastern League opener on May 15, 1909. The Bay Street ball grounds were home to Rochester's teams from 1907 to 1928. The crowd was so large that it spilled over into the outfield area. (Courtesy of the Albert R. Stone Negative Collection, Rochester Museum and Science Center.)

LIMBERING UP. An unidentified Rochester player loosens up before a 1920 game. (Courtesy of the Albert R. Stone Negative Collection, Rochester Museum and Science Center.)

WARNING TRACK PARKING. Spectators were occasionally allowed to park their cars in the far reaches of the outfield. (Courtesy of the Albert R. Stone Negative Collection, Rochester Museum and Science Center.)

THE OPENING ACT. The batter prepares to swing as the Rochester Hustlers begin their 1909 season before a packed house at Baseball Park on Bay Street. It was a banner year for the Hustlers, who went on to win the first of three consecutive pennants. (Courtesy of the Albert R. Stone Negative Collection, Rochester Museum and Science Center.)

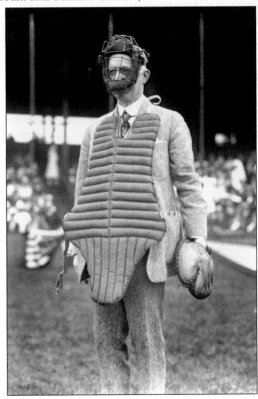

A KODAK MOMENT. George Eastman, founder of the world-famous Eastman Kodak Company, is dressed in a catcher's uniform for pregame ceremonies at Baseball Park on June 23, 1917. Eastman was taking part in the Industrial Rochester Red Cross Field Day. (Courtesy of the Albert R. Stone Negative Collection, Rochester Museum and Science Center.)

SANDLOT SLUGGERS. Surrounded by their teammates, two boys alternate grasping the handle of a baseball bat to determine which team will bat first. The two boys holding the bat are Mike Jacobi (left) and Sam Furioso. The boys are preparing to play in a sandlot game on April 16, 1916. (Courtesy of the Albert R. Stone Negative Collection, Rochester Museum and Science Center.)

THE ENDLESS SUMMER. Rochester Colts manager Arthur Irwin peruses the lineup with captain Henry "Shorty" Long before the season opener at Baseball Park on May 4, 1920. That season, the Colts suffered a franchise record 12-game losing streak on their way to a dismal 45-106 won-lost record. Irwin left to manage Hartford the following summer. According to *The Baseball Encyclopedia*, he died on July 16, 1921, when he either jumped or fell into the Atlantic Ocean during a steamer trip from New York to Boston. A subsequent investigation revealed that Irwin had led a double life for the last 30 years, with a legal wife and son in Hartford and a second, common-law wife in New York City. (Courtesy of the Albert R. Stone Negative Collection, Rochester Museum and Science Center.)

BATTER CHATTER. Two unidentified Rochester players talk to each other while waiting for their turns at bat before a game at Baseball Park *c.* 1920. (Courtesy of the Albert R. Stone Negative Collection, Rochester Museum and Science Center.)

BABE TAKES A BREATHER. Babe Ruth rests with his teammates in the dugout during a July 6, 1921 exhibition game at Baseball Park. (Courtesy of the Albert R. Stone Negative Collection, Rochester Museum and Science Center.)

THE SULTAN GETS IN HIS SWATS. Legendary slugger Babe Ruth displays his powerful swing during a July 6, 1921 exhibition game between the New York Yankees and the Rochester Colts at Baseball Park. (Courtesy of the Albert R. Stone Negative Collection, Rochester Museum and Science Center.)

CLOWNING AROUND. Before Max Patkin, Al Schacht was the clown prince of baseball, entertaining fans in parks throughout America with his zany antics. Prior to his comedic career, Schacht pitched for the 1917 Rochester Hustlers. Some would say his performance was a joke, as he lost 21 of 33 decisions.

RUN, RABBIT, RUN. Baseball Hall of Famer Rabbit Maranville spent the 1927 season with the Rochester Tribe and became an instant hit with the fans. A fun-loving sort, Maranville entertained patrons with his basket catches in the outfield.

THE HAIG. Walter Hagen, the Rochester-born golfing legend who has won more major tournaments than everyone but Jack Nicklaus and Bobby Jones, invested $10,000 to become part owner of the Rochester Tribe in 1927. Hagen's time as an owner was brief. He bailed out after that season, having lost more than $37,000 in the venture. He was saddened that things did not work out because baseball had always been his first love. Hagen had been one of Rochester's top semiprofessional baseball players in the early 1900s. He was so good that the Philadelphia Phillies invited him to spring training, but on the advice of a sports editor, he declined so he could pursue a full-time golfing career.

BRANCHING OUT. Two decades before achieving baseball immortality by signing Jackie Robinson to break the color barrier, Branch Rickey made his impact on Rochester baseball. As general manager of the St. Louis Cardinals, Rickey is credited with creating baseball's first full-fledged farm system for developing players. Before the 1928 season, he identified Rochester as a city with great baseball potential and placed the Cardinals' top minor-league team there. He was also instrumental in getting a new baseball stadium built at 500 Norton Street. Rickey (third from left) is pictured with Gil Hodges (far left), Gene Hermanski (second from left), and Jackie Robinson.

THE MAN IN BLUE. Years before he became a Hall of Fame umpire, Jocko Conlan distinguished himself as a ballplayer. In 1924, Conlan batted .321 and played a solid center field for the Rochester Tribe. Another Hall of Fame umpire with a Flower City connection was Rochester native Bill Klem.

Two
TAKING FLIGHT
WITH THE CARDINALS

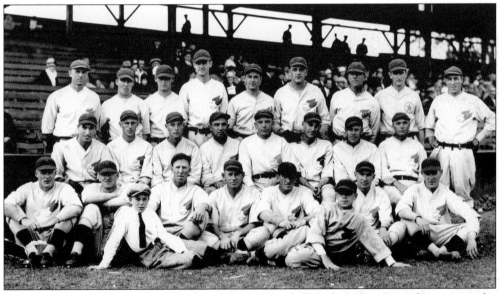

A FOND FAREWELL. The Wings bade goodbye to Baseball Park on Bay Street by winning the 1928 International League pennant. Herman Bell paced the team with 21 wins—two of the victories coming in a doubleheader sweep on the final day of the season to give Rochester the pennant by .001 percentage points.

THE ARCHITECTS. Manager Billy Southworth (left) and general manager Warren Giles laid the foundation for a successful start to the Wings affiliation with the St. Louis Cardinals.

Official Score Card

ROCHESTER RED WING BASEBALL CLUB, Inc.

"RED WINGS"

1928   1928

"BILLY" SOUTHWORTH
Manager

Ride the BLUE BUS
ROCHESTER BATAVIA BUFFALO

SAFETY COACH

BUFFALO, Only $2.00

Every Fan will want to see Rochester and other good teams play at Buffalo. Ride the Blue Bus when you go. Service close to Ball Park down Main Street in Buffalo. Avoid traffic and parking worries.

BUFFALO — Williamsville, Clarence, Akron, Attica, Darien, Batavia, Le Roy, Bergen, Caledonia, Scottsville — **ROCHESTER**

Every hour on the hour

AT BUFFALO	
BALTIMORE	May 2, 3, 4, 5*
NEWARK	May 6†, 7, 8, 9
READING	May 10, 11, 12*, 13†
JERSEY CITY	May 14, 15, 16, 17
MONTREAL	May 18, 19*, 20†, 21
ROCHESTER	May 25, 26*, 27†, 28
TORONTO	May 29, 30‡ A.M.-P.M.
MONTREAL	June 25, 26, 27, 28
TORONTO	July 3, 4‡ A.M.-P.M., 29†
BALTIMORE	July 6, 7*, 8†, 9
READING	July 10, 11, 12, 13
NEWARK	July 14*, 15†, 16, 17
JERSEY CITY	July 18, 19, 20, 21*
ROCHESTER	July 30, 31, Aug. 1, 2
TORONTO	Aug. 5†, Sep. 16†, 21, 22*, 23†
NEWARK	Aug. 20, 21, 22, 23
JERSEY CITY	Aug. 24, 25*, 26-26†
BALTIMORE	Aug. 27, 28, 29-29
READING	Aug. 30, 31, Sept. 1-1*
ROCHESTER	Sept. 3‡ A.M.-P.M., 4, 5
MONTREAL	Sept. 6, 7, 8*, 9†

*Saturdays; †Sundays; ‡Holidays

Terminal—Broad Street and South Ave.—Main 2442

WINGING IT. The 1928 season marked a number of firsts for professional baseball in Rochester. The team signed a working agreement with a major-league team, the St. Louis Cardinals, for the first time. Billy Southworth took over as manager, and Rochester's nickname changed from the Tribe to the Red Wings.

CHRISTENING A NEW BALLPARK. The opening of brand-new Red Wing Stadium on May 2, 1929, was an event worthy of big headlines. Despite a steady rain, 14,885 fans flocked to the ballpark to watch Rochester lose 3-0 to the Reading Keys.

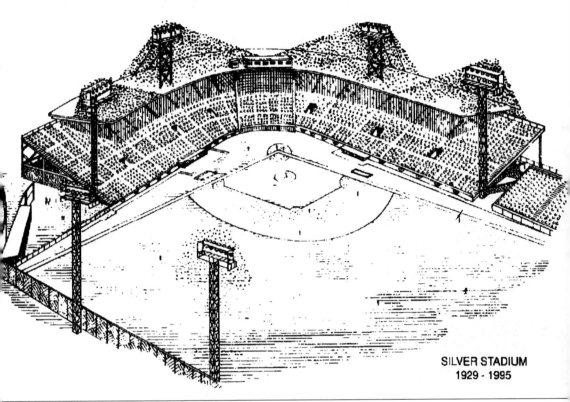

SILVER STADIUM
1929 - 1995

THE TAJ MAHAL OF THE MINOR LEAGUES. That is how people throughout baseball referred to Red Wing Stadium when it opened on May 2, 1929. The ballpark at 500 Norton Street cost $415,000 to construct and served as Rochester's baseball home for 68 years.

JAMES THE RIPPER. In 1930, James "Rip" Collins put together the finest individual season in Rochester baseball history. The switch-hitting first baseman batted .376 with 40 homers, 165 runs scored, and an International League–record 180 RBIs as the Wings won the Junior World Series. That club, which recorded a 105-62 record, is regarded by many as the greatest Rochester team of all time.

SPECS-TACULAR. George "Specs" Toporcer, one of the most popular players in Wings history, spent seven seasons in a Rochester uniform, including three as a player-manager. From 1928 to 1934, he played 880 games for the Wings, establishing club records with 113 stolen bases and 628 runs scored. A two-time International League MVP, the bespectacled second baseman was part of the 1929 infield that turned 225 double plays, setting a professional baseball record that still stands.

36

THE VOICE OF THE WINGS. Gunnar O. Wiig was Rochester's preeminent sportscaster during radio's golden age in the 1920s and 1930s. He is shown here broadcasting a Red Wings game on September 27, 1930. (Courtesy of the Alfred R. Stone Negative Collection, Rochester Museum and Science Center.)

The **Red Wing**

RED WING STADIUM

NEWS

ROCHESTER, N.Y.

Volume 1   Rochester, August 27, 1931   Number 1

TWIN BILL WITH READING HERE SUNDAY

Brilliant Red Wing Graduates

Derringer   Collins

Former Red Wings Vital to Success of Cardinals

Several of the greatest players on the St. Louis Cardinals, National League Champions, are former members of the Rochester Red Wings. In 1929 Charley Gelbert graduated to the Cards, and in 1930 Watkins and Mancuso followed him. This year Collins, Derringer and Martin more than made good with the Na-

Billy Southworth's Red Wings, Champions of the International League, are striving gallantly for their fourth pennant in four seasons and the ninth flag in Rochester's history. Rochester last year equalled Baltimore's record of eight pennants and then topped it off by a victory over the Louisville Colonels, American Association leaders, in the Little World Series.

If the winning spirit has anything to do with it, and it has, the Red Wings stand a fine chance of again bringing home the laurels. In 1928 Billy's team had a teriffic uphill struggle and won only on the last day of the season, and then by one point. In 1929 and last year the Wings' margin was more comfortable.

The Red Wings, although they are now finished with Baltimore and Newark, still have some mighty tough dates on their schedule. The series

DEVELOPING TALENT. As this team newsletter to fans points out, Rochester was instrumental in sending players such as pitcher Paul Derringer and first baseman Rip Collins to the big-league club in St. Louis, where they became solid performers for the Cardinals' famous "Gashouse Gang." (Courtesy of Dan Guilfoyle.)

PLAYING PEPPER. Before joining the Cardinals, Ray Pepper spent five seasons in the Rochester outfield. The .316 batting average he compiled from 1929 to 1933 is sixth highest in Red Wings history, and his record of 419 RBIs is second best. His best season came in 1931, when he hit .356 with 121 RBIs. (Courtesy of the National Baseball Hall of Fame Library.)

A Winning Combination. Baseball Hall of Famer George Sisler (left) and player-manager Billy Southworth helped the Wings repeat their International League pennant in 1931. Sisler, a lifetime .340 hitter who had twice batted over .400 for the lowly St. Louis Browns during a stellar 15-year big-league career, had never pulled on a minor-league uniform until he arrived in Rochester. Southworth managed the Wings to four pennants before his promotion to the Cardinals, whom he guided to World Series titles in 1942 and 1944.

PUSH 'EM UP POOCH. Red Wings Hall of Famer George Puccinelli had a season to remember in 1932. He batted .391 with 28 home runs and 115 RBIs that season, and during one hot stretch, he hit in a club-record 31 consecutive games. The outfielder, known as "Push 'Em Up Pooch," was honored on Italian-American Night and received an automobile from his admirers. Unhappy with the selection of cars, Puccinelli spent $175 of his own money for an upgraded vehicle the next day, an action that angered many Red Wing fans. (Courtesy of the National Baseball Hall of Fame Library.)

SLINGIN' SAMMY'S BASEBALL FLING. Sammy Baugh, one of the greatest quarterbacks in National Football League history, grew up dreaming of becoming the next Babe Ruth. Baugh spent part of the 1938 season playing shortstop for the Red Wings. As his statistics show, he did not exactly set the world on fire in Rochester. In 37 games, Baugh batted just .183 with a home run, a triple, and 11 RBIs. After the season, St. Louis Cardinals general manager Branch Rickey attempted to sign him to another minor-league contract, but Baugh turned down the offer and devoted himself fully to football. It proved to be a wise decision, as Baugh became a Hall of Fame quarterback with the Washington Redskins.

CRABBY. Estel Crabtree played for the Wings from 1933 to 1940, establishing several career club records that may never be broken. He remains Rochester's all-time leader in RBIs (542), hits (1,041), and games played (934). His "miracle" homer in the bottom of the ninth of a September 23, 1939 Governors' Cup game against the Newark Bears remains one of the most significant moments in team history. Crabtree's three-run shot sent the game into extra innings. The Wings won that night and then captured the Governors' Cup the next day.

TWINKLE TOES. George Selkirk, a graduate of Rochester's Edison Tech High School, was acquired by the Wings in 1933 and turned in a superb season, batting .306 with 22 homers and 108 RBIs. The right fielder, known as "Twinkle Toes" because he was light on his feet, went on to play several years with the Yankees, taking over for Babe Ruth in right field.

SIR WALTER. After Walter Alston ripped four hits in his 1937 debut with the Red Wings, some predicted the big first baseman was destined for greatness. He was—as a manager. In his three seasons with Rochester, Alston hit .246, .240, and .158. However, he made his mark as the Dodgers manager, guiding Brooklyn to its only World Series title (1955) and Los Angeles to three more. His achievements as a manager earned him induction into the Baseball Hall of Fame.

WORKING HIS WAY UP. Rochester native Gabe Paul began working for the ball club as a mascot and rose to the position of club secretary by the early 1930s. He later became president of the Cleveland Indians and New York Yankees.

BILLY BALL. Although they finished the 1939 regular season in second place, manager Billy Southworth's Wings were dominant in the postseason, winning the first of the franchise's 10 Governors' Cup titles. Rochester was paced by pitcher Silas Johnson, who led the International League in wins with 22. (Courtesy of Dan Guilfoyle.)

RACKING UP THE Ws. Norbert "Nubs" Kleinke pitched for the Red Wings from 1934 to 1938, winning 70 games, the second-greatest number in franchise history. Twice, Kleinke won 19 or more games in a season. In 2001, he was inducted into the Red Wings Hall of Fame.

(Es)tel Going Strong

By NED WHIT

ESTEL CRABTREE - WINGS' CENTER-
FIELDER - THIS IS HIS EIGHTH
CONSECUTIVE YEAR AS A "RED WING".

"CRABBY"

PAPA
TIME

TIME "OUT" - HE'S 34
BUT YOU WOULDN'T KNOW IT-
HIS BATTING AVERAGE, AS THIS
CARTOON IS DRAWN, IS .319.

WINDING DOWN. Estel "Crabby" Crabtree was still a productive player and a fan favorite as he wound down his eighth and final season with the Wings in 1940. Crabtree finished the year with a .314 batting average.

ANOTHER BANNER YEAR. The Wings managed to win the International League pennant in 1940 despite going through four managers: Billy Southworth, Tony Kaufmann, Estel Crabtree, and Mike Ryba. (Courtesy of Dan Guilfoyle.)

"OLD FOLKS" RYBA. Mike Ryba had been assigned to Rochester to assist manager Billy Southworth as a coach and backup pitcher and catcher. However, Ryba threw the ball so well in spring training that he was put into the rotation. All he did was win 24 of 32 decisions to earn 1940 International League MVP honors.

A LEAP OF FAITH. Hamming it up during a 1940 spring-training session in Florida are, from left to right, Wings infielders Harry Davis, George Fallon, Gene Lillard, and Whitey Kurowski.

PRESIDENTIAL PITCH. Franklin Delano Roosevelt, depicted here on a patriotic Red Wings brochure, asked the commissioner of baseball to continue playing games during World War II. The president believed that baseball could provide a much needed distraction for soldiers and citizens alike. (Courtesy of Pete Dobrovitz.)

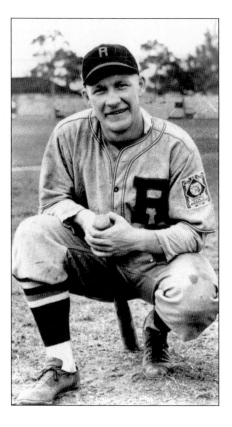

MR. CONSISTENCY. George "Whitey" Kurowski turned in three solid seasons for the Wings while manning the hot corner from 1939 to 1941. His statistics for each season were almost identical: 11 homers, 68 RBIs, .291 in 1939; 15-73-.279 in 1940; and 13-69-.288 in 1941. Kurowski went on to become an All-Star with the St. Louis Cardinals and wound up hitting a pivotal home run as they won the 1942 World Series against the New York Yankees. He was inducted into the Red Wings Hall of Fame in 2000.

STAN THE YOUNG MAN. Stan Musial made his last minor-league stop in Rochester with the Red Wings in 1941, and he did not stay long. He spent just 54 games in Rochester, batting .326 with 10 doubles, 4 triples, 3 homers, and 21 RBIs, before being promoted to the Cardinals. During his Hall of Fame career in St. Louis, the man who became known as "the Man" won seven National League batting titles and three MVP awards. (Courtesy of Pete Dobrovitz.)

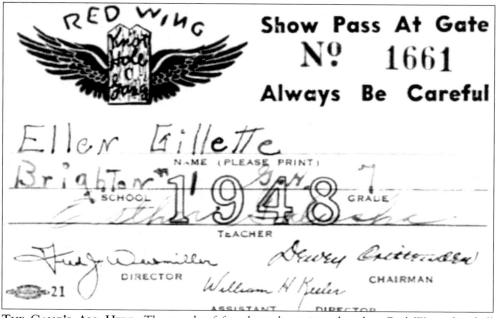

The Gang's All Here. Thousands of fans have been introduced to Red Wings baseball through their membership in the Knothole Gang. The program, which began in Rochester in 1926, allowed young fans to get into games at reduced rates. All you had to do was show your membership card similar to the one pictured here. In the late 1940s, the Knothole Gang was so popular that it spawned a youth band that would perform during games at Red Wing Stadium. (Courtesy of Pete Dobrovitz.)

JACKIE ROBINSON COMES TO TOWN. A season-high crowd of 14,386 showed up at Red Wing Stadium on May 30, 1946, to watch Jackie Robinson play for the Montreal Royals, the top farm club of the Brooklyn Dodgers. The huge throng had hoped to watch Robinson in action. However, the African American player who later helped integrate a sport and a nation sat out the doubleheader against Rochester with a leg injury he had suffered the night before in a game against Buffalo.

THE ROCHESTER AMERICAN-GIANTS. Before Jackie Robinson broke Major League Baseball's color barrier in 1947, African Americans who desired to play professionally had only one option—the Negro Leagues. Like white baseball, the Negro Leagues had their own system of major- and minor-league teams, and one of the minor-league clubs was the Rochester American-Giants. Several members of that club are pictured here before a mid-1940s game against Buffalo. (Courtesy of Roxie Sinkler.)

51

PACKED HOUSES. The Red Wings, like baseball teams throughout America, enjoyed a resurgence in attendance after World War II. In 1949, Rochester drew 443,536 fans, a franchise attendance record that lasted for 58 years.

THE BIG BOPPER. In parts of six seasons with the Wings, left-handed hitter Russ Derry established himself as the most prolific slugger in team history. With a swing that was tailor made for the short right-field fence at Red Wing Stadium, Derry established franchise records for most homers in a season (42 in 1949) and a career (134). The two-time International League home run champion was a member of the inaugural class of the Red Wings Hall of Fame in 1989.

THE 1949 ROCHESTER RED WINGS

Al Stringer Cloyd Boyer John Grodyocke Tom Poholsky Ralph Lapointe Ed Mierkowicz Johnny Lukas

Dick Bokelmann Dave Richmond Steve Bilko George Copeland Russ Derry Kenton Boyer Don Munns Bert Hall Don Thompson

Hank Edwards Charlie Marshall Eddie Blake Dick Burgett Johny Keane Erv Dusak Dick Cole Dave Thomas John Bucha Danny White

POWER BROKERS. Although they did not win the pennant, the 1949 Wings were quite successful and entertaining. Paced by the slugging of Russ Derry (42 homers) and Steve Bilko (34 homers) and the pitching of Cloyd Boyer and Tom Poholsky, Rochester finished in second place with an 85-67 record.

JOHN ANTONELLI

LOCAL HERO. Johnny Antonelli, a star pitcher at Rochester's Jefferson High School, signed for a huge bonus with the Boston Braves at age 18. However, he wound up gaining major-league fame with the New York Giants. He had his best season in 1954, when he went 21-7 and led the National League in winning percentage (.750) and ERA (2.30). He picked up a win and a save as the Giants swept the Cleveland Indians that October in the World Series. Antonelli compiled a 126-110 record with a 3.34 ERA during his 12 years in the big leagues.

ATHLETIC SUPPORTERS. Of the millions of fans who have watched the Wings play, Red Smith may have been the most vociferous and Bill Nill the most devoted. Smith (doffing his cap) was a sports barker who announced lineups through a megaphone at Rochester-area sports events before the advent of public address systems. He became a fixture at Red Wing Stadium, where even into his 80s, he could be seen roaming the stands with the aid of a cane, leading various sections of the park in cheers. Nill, a locksmith, attended his first game in 1909 at Baseball Park on Bay Street and later became a diehard at Red Wing Stadium. The only three home games he missed in 69 years were the ones played while he was off fighting World War II. So deep was his devotion that when Nill died in August 1978, his widow, Pat, spread his ashes beneath the stands at Silver Stadium.

PENNANT FEVER. Managed by Johnny Keane and paced by league MVP Tom Poholsky and batting champion Don Richmond, the 1950 Red Wings won the International League pennant by seven games but wound up losing to the Baltimore Orioles in the finals. (Courtesy of Dan Guilfoyle.)

SCORECARD
Rochester
RED WINGS
INTERNATIONAL LEAGUE CHAMPIONS 1950
GOLDEN ANNIVERSARY 1951
NATIONAL ASSOCIATION
Price 10¢

TWO-TIMER. Don Richmond won back-to-back International League batting titles, hitting .333 in 1950 and .350 the following year. During his six-year career with the team, he smacked 857 hits, the third best in franchise history, and finished with a career .327 batting average. He never hit below .296 in a Rochester uniform. (Courtesy of Pete Dobrovitz.)

AN *EXTRA* SPECIAL DUEL. On August 13, 1950, Red Wings pitcher Tom Poholsky beat Jersey City's Andy Tomasic in one of the greatest pitching matchups in baseball history. Each man went the distance—22 innings—as the Wings won 3-2. Poholsky yielded 10 hits, walked five, and struck out five to pick up the win. He finished the season with 18 wins and an International League best 2.17 ERA. Poholsky went 32-16 in two seasons with Rochester and was inducted into the Red Wings Hall of Fame in 1990. (Courtesy of the National Baseball Hall of Fame Library.)

Vern Rapp · Niles Jordan · Allie Clark · Orlando Rubert · [illegible]/TRAINER · George Condrick · Les Fusselman · Jack Pierron · Bob Hoch

Charlie Kress · Lou Ortig · Ed Murkowsky · Don Richmond · Harry Hartman · Bobby Tiefenauer · Jack Faszholz · Tom Burgess

Dennis Reeder · Wally Moon · Joy Kahn · Harry Walker/MANAGER · Cot Deal · Vern Benson · Jack Huesman

RED-HOT WINGS. From August 26 through September 12, 1953, the Wings won a franchise record 19 straight games. Pitcher Cot Deal posted four victories during the streak but also suffered the loss in the game that halted it. The victory splurge was part of a 29-3 stretch that enabled the Wings to clinch the 1953 International League pennant.

GOING TO BAT FOR SPECS. Wings fans were saddened by the news that former Rochester player and manager Specs Toporcer had become blind. In an effort to honor him and defray the medical expenses incurred from several eye operations, the Wings arranged for an exhibition game between the St. Louis Cardinals and Boston Red Sox at Red Wing Stadium on July 21, 1952. (Courtesy of Gary Siwicki.)

THE MAD HATTER. Former National League batting champion Harry "the Hat" Walker guided the Wings to a Governors' Cup title in 1952 and an International League pennant in 1953. He went on to manage three different big-league teams. (Courtesy of the National Baseball Hall of Fame Library.)

THIS BUCK STOPPED HERE. The late great Jack Buck spent the 1953 season as the Red Wings play-by-play announcer before heading to St. Louis, where he became the voice of the Cardinals. Known for his gravelly voice and memorable calls, Buck was inducted into the broadcasters' wing of the Baseball Hall of Fame in Cooperstown.

PRACTICING WHAT HE PREACHED. Nicknamed "the Preacher," Jack Faszholz established himself as the winningest pitcher in Wings history, recording 80 victories in seven seasons. His best year was 1954, when he went 18-9 with a 3.21 ERA. A member of three Governors' Cup champions, Faszholz was inducted into the Red Wings Hall of Fame in 1990.

A GOOD DEAL. Inducted into the Red Wings Hall of Fame in 1994, Ellis "Cot" Deal ranks as the fifth winningest pitcher in team history, with 61 victories. A member of three Governors' Cup championship teams in the 1950s, Deal occasionally played the outfield on his non-pitching days because he was an excellent hitter and fielder. Deal also managed the Wings from 1957 to 1958.

MEASURING UP. Pitcher Tony Jacobs was virtually unbeatable for two full seasons, posting a 28-4 record for the 1952 and 1953 Wings. A member of the Red Wings Hall of Fame, Jacobs went 12-3 with a 2.63 ERA in 1953 and 16-1 with a 2.91 ERA in 1954.

BAT MAN. A member of the Red Wings Hall of Fame, Allie Clark batted over .300 three times in his five seasons in Rochester during the 1950s.

BREAKING DOWN BARRIERS. On June 30, 1954, Thomas Edison Alston became the first African American to play for the Red Wings, after he was demoted to Rochester by the St. Louis Cardinals. Alston, pictured here with former Cardinals' owner August Busch, batted .297 with 7 homers and 42 RBIs in 79 games with the Wings. He was recalled by the Cardinals later that season and filled a reserve role. During the next three summers, he yo-yoed between the majors and minors before being released. His life after baseball was a sad one. He attempted to commit suicide on several occasions and spent parts of 10 years in a mental institution.

HONORING CRABBY. On July 19, 1957, the Red Wings honored Estel Crabtree at Red Wing Stadium. Former New York Giants pitching great Carl Hubbell (left) was on hand, as was baseball's all-time batting average leader, Ty Cobb (center).

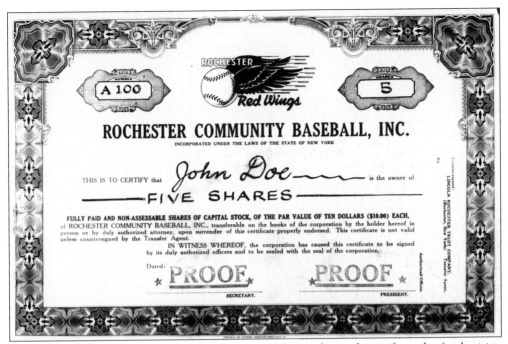

TAKING STOCK IN THE WINGS. Pictured is one of the stock certificates from the fund-raising drive that saved minor-league baseball in Rochester in the 1950s.

CREDIT HIM WITH THE SAVE. He made a living as a music store owner, but he made his mark as the head of Rochester Community Baseball. Morrie Silver came up with the idea for the stock drive that saved professional baseball in Rochester in the mid-1950s. He returned in the early 1960s and helped bail the financially strapped franchise out again. Silver worked for a token salary of $1 a year, often saying, "The Rochester fans and their love of baseball is my pay." In 1968, the community paid its respects in another way, renaming the ballpark at 500 Norton Street "Silver Stadium."

A FINAL TUNE-UP FOR GIBBY. The last superstar to emerge from the Red Wings–Cardinals marriage was Bob Gibson. The Baseball Hall of Famer pitched in 20 games for the Wings in 1958, going 5-5 with a 2.45 ERA. After posting a 3-5 won-lost record with St. Louis in 1959, Gibson returned to Rochester and went 2-3 with a 2.85 ERA. He went on to win 251 games and two Cy Young Awards during his 17-year big-league career. (Courtesy of Dan Mason.)

CATCHING ON QUICKLY. Tim McCarver, who gained fame as a big-league catcher and network baseball broadcaster, had a brief stint with the Wings, batting a robust .357 in 17 games before his promotion to the St. Louis Cardinals during the summer of 1959.

66

AND THE WINNER IS. For nearly a quarter of a century, the Hickok Belt was considered the Oscar of professional sports. It was presented annually to America's top professional athlete at an Academy Awards–style gala hosted by the Rochester Press-Radio Club. The belt was made of alligator skin and contained a solid gold buckle along with an encrusted four-carat diamond and 26 gem chips. The award was presented from 1950 to 1976. (Courtesy of the Tony Wells Agency.)

A PERFECT FIT. New York Yankees center fielder Mickey Mantle tries on the Hickok Belt he won in 1956 as Alan Hickok looks on. (Courtesy of the Tony Wells Agency.)

AN ALL-STAR LINEUP. Willie Mays, the winner of the 1954 Hickok Belt, is joined by a group of baseball All-Stars. From left to right are Roy Campanella, Larry Doby, Phil Rizzuto, Yogi Berra, Johnny Antonelli, Mays, Bob Keegan, and Wally Moon. (Courtesy of the Tony Wells Agency.)

A DOUBLEHEADER. Los Angeles Dodgers pitching legend Sandy Koufax was the only two-time winner, garnering honors in 1963 and 1965. (Courtesy of the Tony Wells Agency.)

ROGER AND FRIEND. The winner of the 1961 Hickok Belt, Roger Maris, shares his special moment with a young fan. (Courtesy of the Tony Wells Agency.)

CAMPY'S TURN. Brooklyn Dodgers catcher Roy Campanella (center) and Rochester golf legend Sam Urzetta (right) share a light moment with Ray Hickok during the 1955 dinner. (Courtesy of the Tony Wells Agency.)

SAY HEY. Willie Mays, the "Say Hey Kid," visits with Hall of Fame catchers Yogi Berra (left) and Roy Campanella (right) at the 1955 Day of Champions dinner. (Courtesy of the Tony Wells Agency.)

YAZ. Carl Yastrzemski (left), the 1967 Hickok Belt winner, poses with Alan Hickok. (Courtesy of the Tony Wells Agency.)

A LOCAL BOY MAKES GOOD. Born and bred in Rochester, Bob Keegan spent six seasons in the major leagues with the Chicago White Sox and realized a pitcher's dream during the summer of 1957 when he threw a no-hitter. After going 0-2 with the White Sox the following summer, Keegan returned to his hometown and wound up finishing his professional baseball career there. In 1959, he led the International League with 18 victories. He won six more games the following season before retiring. He was inducted into the Red Wings Hall of Fame in 1993.

A COMMUNITY EFFORT. Baseball in Rochester fell on hard times in the late 1950s, and it appeared as if the financially strapped Red Wings might have to leave town. However, club president Morrie Silver initiated a stock drive, and 8,222 Rochesterians responded by purchasing $10 certificates to save the Wings.

FLYING THE COOP. Nineteen sixty marked the final year that Rochester was affiliated with the St. Louis Cardinals. The logo on this spring-training brochure features Princess Red Wing, the team's longtime mascot.

Three
SOARING WITH
THE ORIOLES

FIRST EDITION. The 1961 season was the first year that the Red Wings were the Triple-A farm club of the Baltimore Orioles. That team, under the guidance of manager Clyde King, finished in fourth place in the International League. Among the notable players were sluggers Boog Powell and Luke Easter (back row, fifth and sixth from the left, respectively).

A HUMONGOUS STAR. The first big star of the Orioles–Red Wings affiliation was John "Boog" Powell, a 6-foot 4-inch, 230-pound first baseman and outfielder who conjured memories of past Rochester sluggers Russ Derry, Steve Bilko, and Johnny Mize. In 1961, his only season with the Wings, Powell batted .321 with 93 RBIs and an International League–leading 32 home runs. Powell went on to become one of the most feared sluggers in baseball, smacking 339 home runs during his 17-year big-league career.

Nothing Quirky about This. Wings first baseman Boog Powell (No. 29) shakes hands with Art Quirk after the pitcher gets the final out of a seven-inning no-hitter against the Syracuse Chiefs on July 4, 1961. It was the highlight of a career that saw Quirk post a 17-14 record in his two seasons with Rochester. (Courtesy of Dan Guilfoyle.)

Here's the Scoop. First baseman Boog Powell reaches for a throw. (Courtesy of Pete Dobrovitz.)

SOMEWHERE OVER THE RAINBOW. Jim "Mugsy" Finigan, a light-hitting second baseman, earned a permanent spot in Red Wing lore on September 11, 1961, when he delivered four hits and drove in six runs, including the game-winner, to defeat the Toronto Maple Leafs and secure a spot in the Governor's Cup playoffs. Finigan's shocking two-run homer to send the game into extra innings became known as Finigan's Rainbow, a takeoff on *Finian's Rainbow,* a popular early-1960s Broadway musical. Finigan retired from baseball after that season, following a contract dispute with the Wings, and never played professionally again. (Courtesy of Pete Dobrovitz.)

A GIANT AT BAT. Wings first baseman Luke Easter shows the batting stance that terrified many a pitcher.

THE GOSPEL ACCORDING TO LUKE.
Although Luke Easter was past his prime, few players ever captivated a city the way he did Rochester. A mountain of a man at 6 feet 4 inches and 250 pounds, "Big Luke" was as exciting swinging and missing as he was hitting balls over the light towers. He was a gentle giant with an infectious smile and engaging sense of humor. The Wings acquired him in 1959 from Buffalo for the paltry sum of $100. He spent parts of six seasons with the team as a player, coach, and goodwill ambassador. It was one of the best investments the Wings ever made.

THE GOOD HUMOR MAN. Longtime sportswriter George Beahon wrote that cheery Luke Easter was always making new friends for the ball club.

M'M, M'M, GOOD. While playing in Rochester, Luke Easter started up his own sausage company. Here, he is shown sampling his product.

BUSH-LEAGUE FOLK HEROES. Steve Bilko, one of the legendary sluggers in minor-league history, watches Steve Dalkowski, one of the legendary pitchers in minor-league history, warm up. Bilko spent six seasons with the Wings. His best year was in 1949, when he hit .310 with 34 homers and 125 RBIs. Dalkowski was regarded as the hardest-throwing pitcher of all time, but he could not control his blazing fastball and never made it to the big leagues.

SLUGGING SAM. Outfielder Sam Bowens had a big year for the Wings in 1963, batting .287 with 22 homers and 70 RBIs.

THE VOICE OF AUTHORITY. Joe Cullinane broadcast more Red Wings games than any other announcer did. Known for his down-home charm and storytelling ability, Cullinane was behind the microphone from 1962 to 1974. He was inducted into the Red Wings Hall of Fame in 1995.

AN INAUSPICIOUS DEBUT. A crowd of 14,156 went home disappointed as the Red Wings opened their 1963 season at Red Wing Stadium with a 17-5 loss to Arkansas.

1964 ROCHESTER RED WINGS

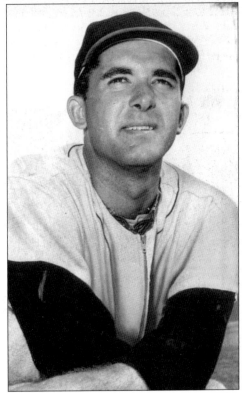

A PHOTO FINISH. Manager Darrell Johnson's 1964 Wings clinched a playoff spot on the final day of the season as pitcher Mike McCormick (right) hit a home run and shut out the Buffalo Bisons 1-0. Despite being a fourth-place finisher, the Wings went on to win the Governor's Cup.

STAN THE MAN RETURNS. On June 28, 1964, Stan Musial (center) returned to Red Wing Stadium for a day in his honor. Musial donned a Red Wings uniform and took part in an old-timers game.

MOWING THEM DOWN. He never drove in a run or made a diving catch, but Dick Sierens (seated on tractor) was a solid contributor to Rochester's baseball success, serving as the Silver Stadium groundskeeper for more than half a century. His behind-the-scenes work was recognized in 1991, when he was inducted into the Red Wings Hall of Fame.

A POTENT INFIELD. Before the 1966 season, Red Wings manager Earl Weaver (No. 4) poses on the steps of the dugout with his starting infielders. Clockwise from the left are first baseman Mike Epstein, third baseman Steve Demeter, shortstop Mark Belanger, and second baseman Mickey McGuire.

CELEBRATION TIME. Feisty Red Wings manager Earl Weaver receives a champagne shower after his team clinched the International League pennant in 1966. Weaver spent two seasons in Rochester, skippering the Wings to 163 victories. After leaving the Flower City, Weaver managed the Baltimore Orioles to one World Series championship and four American League pennants and was inducted into the Baseball Hall of Fame.

SMASHING DEBUT. In his first season as Wings manager, Earl Weaver guided the 1966 team to the International League pennant with an 83-64 record.

A FLAG RAISING. Before the 1967 season opener at Silver Stadium, Red Wings second baseman Mickey McGuire (left), team president Morrie Silver (center), and manager Earl Weaver show off the International League pennant Rochester won the year before.

A COOL PERFORMER AT THE HOT CORNER. Steve Demeter, shown being interviewed by Red Wings announcer Joe Cullinane, was a model of consistency during his five seasons playing third base for the Wings. His best year was 1966, when he batted .313 with 18 homers and 82 RBIs.

POWER SOURCE. Muscular first baseman Mike Epstein helped slug the Wings to the 1966 pennant with a .309 batting average and a league-leading 29 homers and 102 RBIs. The gaudy numbers resulted in him being named International League MVP.

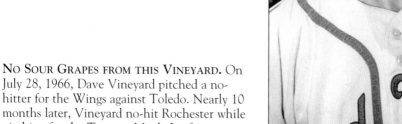

NO SOUR GRAPES FROM THIS VINEYARD. On July 28, 1966, Dave Vineyard pitched a no-hitter for the Wings against Toledo. Nearly 10 months later, Vineyard no-hit Rochester while pitching for the Toronto Maple Leafs.

THE PALMER METHOD. Baseball Hall of Fame pitcher Jim Palmer was sent to the Wings by Baltimore for rehabilitation assignments twice during his career. His ERA took a beating each time—as evidenced by his 11.57 mark in 1967 and his 13.50 figure the following summer. While in Rochester, Palmer yielded the only grand slam of his illustrious baseball career. Interestingly, it was hit by another future Hall of Famer, catcher Johnny Bench, who was playing for the Buffalo Bisons at the time. Rochester was also the place where the long-running feud between Palmer and Earl Weaver began, and it was a result of the down-the-pike pitch the manager ordered Palmer to deliver to Bench. (Courtesy of the National Baseball Hall of Fame Library.)

BEANBALL. The scariest moment in Rochester baseball history occurred during an August 3, 1969 game at Silver Stadium, when Tidewater Tides pitcher Larry Bearnarth fractured the skull of Red Wings utility infielder Chico Fernandez with an unintentional wild pitch. Fernandez fell into a coma and needed emergency surgery to save his life. He recovered completely, and although his playing career ended prematurely, he spent nearly three decades as a minor-league instructor in the Los Angeles Dodgers organization.

LIKE FATHER, LIKE SON. Cal Ripken Sr. spent two seasons managing the Wings, guiding them to a fifth-place finish in 1969 and a third-place finish in 1970. Here, he operates a water fountain at Silver Stadium for his son, Cal Ripken Jr. A decade later, the younger Ripken played for the Wings, earning 1981 International League Rookie of the Year honors. (Courtesy of Pete Dobrovitz.)

THE DON OF ROCHESTER. Long before he became a star player and respected manager in the big leagues, Don Baylor honed his skills with the Wings. His best season was in 1970, when he hit 22 homers, drove in 107 runs, and batted .327. He ranks seventh all-time among Wings players in batting average (.315) and eighth in stolen bases (52).

ROGER AND OUT. He was regarded as the top prospect in the Baltimore Orioles organization, and in 1970, Roger Freed showed why. He batted .334 with 24 homers and 130 RBIs to win Minor League Player of the Year honors. However, Freed wound up being expendable because the Orioles had two other future stars in Bobby Grich and Don Baylor. Freed was dealt to the Philadelphia Phillies after his MVP season and wound up having a brief major-league career.

First Row (l. to r.): Greg Weston, (Visiting Bat Boy), George Farson, Bob Grich, Don Fazio, Mickey Scott, Sam Parrilla, Fred Beene, Jim Knipper (Bat Boy).

Middle Row (l. to r.): Jim Hutto, Mike Ferraro, Terry Crowley, Pete Ward (Coach), Joe Cullinane (Announcer), Joe Altobelli (Manager), Rich Coggins, Orlando Pena, Bill Kirkpatrick, John Oates.

Back Row (l. to r.): Rudy Owen (Trainer), Don Baylor, George Manz, John Montague, Ray Miller, Larry Johnson, Rick Delgado, Roric Harrison, Bill Burbach, Ron Shelton, Herman Schneider (Ass't. Trainer).

THE DREAM TEAM. They started 0-5 and were a .500 team after 66 games, but the 1971 Red Wings were a special group. They finished 86-54 and outlasted the Denver Bears in a seven-game Junior World Series, with all seven games played at Silver Stadium. The club was named one of the greatest teams in minor-league history by *Baseball America* magazine.

THE DYNAMIC DUO. Don Baylor (left) and Bobby Grich were the heart and soul of the 1971 Wings, arguably the best team in Rochester baseball history. First-round draft picks of the Baltimore Orioles, Baylor and Grich lived up to their advance billing. During that memorable 1971 campaign, Grich batted a league-leading .336 with 32 homers and 83 RBIs, while Baylor hit .313 with 20 homers and 95 RBIs.

LITTLE BIG MAN. He stood 5 feet 8 inches and weighed 160 pounds soaking wet, but Freddie Beene was a huge presence on the pitcher's mound. Despite a sore elbow, he went 7-1 for Rochester's Junior World Series champions in 1971, winning some crucial games during the playoffs. He compiled a 46-20 record (.697 winning percentage) in his six-year career with the Wings. He was inducted into the Red Wings Hall of Fame in 1991.

SOWING HIS OATES. Catcher Johnny Oates was an important contributor to that great 1971 team, hitting .277 with 7 homers and 44 RBIs. Despite having to commute to and from Fort Devens, Massachusetts, where he was fulfilling his commitment as an army reservist, Oates batted .529 in the Junior World Series against Denver.

THE SPECIAL K MAN. On July 12, 1971, Red Wings right-hander Roric Harrison set a franchise record by striking out 18 Toledo Mud Hens in a 4-1 win in front of 10,007 fans at Silver Stadium. Harrison added an RBI single and scored another run. He fanned at least one Mud Hen in every inning and balked home the only run against him. He went on to win International League Pitcher of the Year honors that season, going 15-5 with a 2.81 ERA.

SECOND TO NONE. Bobby Grich, shown here playing second base during an Orioles exhibition at Silver Stadium, was inducted into the Red Wings Hall of Fame in 1989.

SATCHEL AT SILVER. Negro League pitching legend Satchel Paige came to Silver Stadium on June 5, 1971, to put on a clinic for youth-league baseball players.

FROM SILVER STADIUM TO THE SILVER SCREEN. Ron Shelton, an infielder with the 1970 and 1971 Wings, never made it to the big leagues in baseball. He did, however, make it to the big time in Hollywood. Shelton's Oscar-nominated comedy, *Bull Durham*, was based on his minor-league experiences, including his seasons in Rochester. The film, starring Kevin Costner (shown below on the set with Shelton), is regarded by many as the best baseball movie ever made.

CHAMPAGNE SHOWER. Manager Joe Altobelli let the bubbly fly after the 1971 Wings clinched the Junior World Series title to become champions of the minor leagues.

THE MICK PAYS A VISIT. On July 25, 1972, Mickey Mantle paid a visit to Silver Stadium for a clinic and home-run-hitting contest. Although he had been retired for four years, the Yankees Hall of Fame center fielder put on a show for a packed house of more than 10,000 spectators, clubbing four homers in 10 pitches to easily beat Joe Altobelli, who is pictured here with Mantle.

FEAST OR FAMINE. Fans knew they were going to get their money's worth every time Jim Fuller came to the plate during the 1973 season. The big outfielder with the muttonchop sideburns and the powerful swing cracked 39 home runs that summer but also set a Red Wings record for whiffing with 197 strikeouts.

A LEGENDARY REUNION. Luke Easter (left) and Steve Bilko (right) flank Bowie Kuhn, Major League Baseball commissioner, before a June 26, 1975 game at Silver Stadium. Easter and Bilko were back for an old-timers game. Kuhn was on hand to present Rochester with an award for being the top organization in minor-league baseball.

FLANNY. Mike Flanagan, a southpaw from New Hampshire, won 79 percent of his decisions during his two seasons with the Wings. After starting 6-1 with a 2.12 ERA, he earned a promotion to Baltimore. He went on to win 141 games and the 1979 Cy Young Award for the Orioles.

ACHIEVING PERFECTION. The only perfect game thrown by a Red Wing took place on August 16, 1974, when Gary Robson retired all 21 batters he faced (and struck out 11) in a 2-0 victory over Charleston in the second game of a doubleheader at Silver Stadium. Under International League rules, doubleheaders consisted of two seven-inning games.

MARTINEZ THE MAGNIFICENT. Dennis Martinez, a right-hander from Granada, Nicaragua, won the International League's pitching Triple Crown in 1976. Martinez topped the International League in wins (14), ERA (2.50) and strikeouts (140).

FAST EDDIE. Future Baseball Hall of Famer Eddie Murray, shown here during a 1987 exhibition game at Silver Stadium, spent just 54 games with the Wings before his promotion to Baltimore in 1976. The switch-hitting first baseman made a lasting impression during his brief stay in Rochester, batting .274 with 11 homers and 40 RBIs.

THE MUSIC MAN. Organist Fred Costello, shown here before a 1982 game at Silver Stadium, has entertained Wings fans for three decades.

TOM TERRIFIC. Tom Kelly, a first baseman and outfielder on loan from the Minnesota Twins, turned in an outstanding season, batting .289 with 18 homers and 70 RBIs in 1976. Kelly went on to gain fame as a big-league manager, leading the Twins to World Series titles in 1987 and 1991.

A HIGH-WIRE ACT. On May 12, 1976, at Silver Stadium, 71-year-old Karl Wallenda successfully negotiated a 500-foot-long tightrope from the center-field fence to the grandstand

roof—61 feet above ground. The performance must have inspired the Wings, as they swept their doubleheader from the Pawtucket Red Sox.

STUFFING SILVER. An overflow crowd of 12,530 watches a Red Wings game at Silver Stadium on August 23, 1980.

A FRANK MANAGER. On May 3, 1978, Baseball Hall of Famer Frank Robinson became the first African American manager in Wings history, replacing Ken Boyer. It was not a fun summer for the only player to win MVP awards in both major leagues, as the powerless Wings finished sixth.

THE IRON KID. The most famous alumnus of the Orioles–Red Wings affiliation was baseball's all-time iron man—Cal Ripken Jr. He spent the 1981 season with the Wings, batting .288 with 23 homers and 73 RBIs. The man who played in a record 2,632 consecutive games with Baltimore was streaky in Rochester, too, not missing a start in 114 games with the Wings before his promotion.

Red Sox 3, Red Wings 2										
Rochester	ab	r	b	bi	**Pawtucket**		ab	r	b	bi
Eaton 2b	10	0	3	0	Graham cf		14	0	1	0
Williams cf	13	0	0	0	Barrett 2b		12	1	2	0
Ripken 3b	13	0	2	0	Walker lf		14	1	2	0
Corey dh	5	1	1	0	Laribee dh		11	0	0	1
Chism ph	1	0	0	0	Koza 1b		14	1	5	1
Rayford c	5	0	0	0	Boggs 3b		12	0	4	1
Logan 1b	12	0	4	0	Bowen rf		12	0	2	0
Valle 1b	1	0	0	0	Gedman c		3	0	1	0
Bourjos lf	4	0	2	1	Ongarato		1	0	0	0
Hale ph	7	0	1	0	LaFrancois		8	0	2	0
Smith lf	0	0	0	0	Valdez ss		13	0	2	0
Hazewood rf	4	0	0	0						
Hart ph	6	0	1	0						
Bonner ss	12	1	3	0						
Huppert c	11	0	1	1						
Putman ph	1	0	0	0						
Grilli p	0	0	0	0						
Speck p	0	0	0	0						
Total	105	2	18	2	**Total**		114	3	21	3

Rochester	000	000	100	000	000	000	001	000	000	000—2
Pawtucket	000	000	001	000	000	000	001	000	000	001—3

No outs when winning run scored.
E—Eaton, Logan, Bonner, Valdez. DP—Rochester 4, Pawtucket 3. LOB—Rochester 30, Pawtucket 23. 2B—Koza 2, Walker, Boggs, Huppert. SB—Eaton. S—Williams 2, Logan, Hart, Huppert 2. SF—Laribee.

Rochester	IP	H	R	ER	BB	SO
Jones	8 2-3	7	1	1	2	5
Schneider	5 1-3	2	0	0	0	8
Luebber	8	6	1	1	2	4
Umbarger	10	4	0	0	0	9
Grilli L, 0-3	0	1	1	1	1	0
Speck	0	1	0	0	0	0
Pawtucket						
Parks	6	3	1	1	4	3
Aponte	4	0	0	0	2	9
Sarmiento	4	3	0	0	2	3
Smithson	3 2-3	2	0	0	3	5
Remmerswaal	4 1-3	4	1	1	3	3
Finch	5	3	0	0	1	3
Hurst	5	2	0	0	3	7
Ojeda W, 9-5	1	1	0	0	0	1

Parks pitched to 3 batters in the 7th.
Grilli pitched to 3 batters in the 33rd.
Speck pitched to 1 batter in the 33rd.
HBP—By Schneider (Laribee). By Parks (Eaton). By Aponte (Bonner), by Grilli (Barrett).
WP—Jones, Hurst, Smithson. T—8:25. A—1,740

ROCHESTER RED WINGS 000 | 000 | 100 | 000 | 000 | 000 | 000 | 000 | 001 | 000 | 000 | 000 | 001 | 001 | 000 | 000 | 001 2

PAWTUCKET RED SOX 000 | 000 | 001 | 000 | 000 | 000 | 000 | 000 | 000 | 000 | 000 | 000 | 000 | 001 | 000 | 000 | 001 3

THE MARATHON GAME. The longest game in baseball history—a 33-inning marathon between the Red Wings and Pawtucket Red Sox—began on April 18, 1981, at McCoy Stadium in Rhode Island and ended there 65 days later. The PawSox wound up winning 3-2 in the bottom of the 33rd. Fourteen pitchers combined to throw more than 1,000 pitches, striking out 60 batters and teaming up for 29 scoreless innings. Rochester center fielder Dallas Williams failed to get a hit in 13 at-bats—the worst single-game batting line in baseball history. Cal Ripken Jr. went 2-13, while counterpart Wade Boggs was 4-12. The cap of losing pitcher Steve Grilli is on display at the Baseball Hall of Fame in Cooperstown.

HIS ACHING KNEES. In one of the game's greatest endurance feats, Red Wings catcher Dave Huppert caught 31 of 33 innings during baseball's longest game.

HERE COMES THE BRIDE. On September 1, 1982, Red Wings catcher Tim Derryberry and Cheryl Toxey were married in a home plate ceremony at Silver Stadium. Several wedding ceremonies were conducted at the old ballpark through the years.

A SNOW JOB. Wings general managers Bob Gaughan (left) and Bill Terlecky (center) join groundskeeper Dick Sierens in the Silver Stadium stands after the 1983 home opener was snowed out.

PERSISTENT PITCHER. Mike Boddicker spent parts of five seasons with the Wings, winning 10 or more games three times. His persistence paid off; in 1984, he was a 20-game winner for the Baltimore Orioles.

UNABLE TO MANAGE. Frank Verdi, shown here arguing with umpire Mike Holoka during a 1985 game, could not buy a break during his time managing the Wings. His 1984 club finished with the worst record in Wings history, and after a 16-40 start the following season, the former Rochester player-coach was fired.

BROWN-BAGGING IT. During the lean years in the mid-1980s, attendance declined, and those who did show up at Silver Stadium occasionally wore disguises.

ARRESTING NIGHT AT SILVER. During a May 29, 1986 game at Silver Stadium, Maine shortstop Corey Snyder flung his bat in disgust toward his dugout after flying out to center. The bat struck and injured two fans in the stands, and Snyder was later charged with two counts of third-degree assault. Nearly two years after the incident, the parties settled out of court. The victims reportedly received $50,000.

DIFFERENT POSITION, SAME RESULT. Johnny Oates, who starred as a catcher on the Wings' 1971 Junior World Series team, returned to Silver as a manager 17 years later and guided Rochester to the Governors' Cup.

HOISTING THE SILVER AT SILVER. Members of the 1988 Wings celebrate in front of the home folks after winning the eighth Governors' Cup in franchise history.

DREAMS DASHED. Mike Jones, one of the best high-school pitchers ever to come out of the Rochester area, was a first-round pick of the Kansas City Royals and seemed destined for greatness until a nearly fatal car accident short-circuited his career. Here, Jones is shown trying to make a comeback while pitching for the Red Wings in 1989.

SWEET SWINGER. Outfielder Steve Finley won the 1988 International League batting title with a .314 average.

Four

ENTERING A

NEW FRONTIER

DELIVERING THE GOODS. A decade before sharing World Series MVP honors with his Arizona Diamondbacks teammate Randy Johnson, Curt Schilling honed his pitching skills with the Red Wings at Silver Stadium. He went 13-11 with a 3.21 ERA in 1989 and was 4-4 with a 3.92 ERA the next year before being promoted by the Baltimore Orioles.

DANIEL BOONE WAS A MAN. His name was Daniel Boone, and, yes, he was related to the legendary frontiersman of the same name (a seventh-generation nephew, to be exact). This Daniel Boone, however, made a name for himself by tossing a no-hitter for the Rochester Red Wings on July 23, 1990, at Silver Stadium.

GETTING A GRIP. Red Wings pitcher Daniel Boone displays the knuckleball grip he used to toss his 1990 no-hitter.

HORN OF PLENTY. On June 23–24, 1990, Sam Horn experienced one of the greatest power surges in Red Wings history. The large slugger hit 3 home runs (including a grand slam) in a doubleheader against Tidewater and then slammed a pair of 3-run homers the following day. That gave him 5 homers and 14 RBIs in 8 at-bats in a 21-hour period.

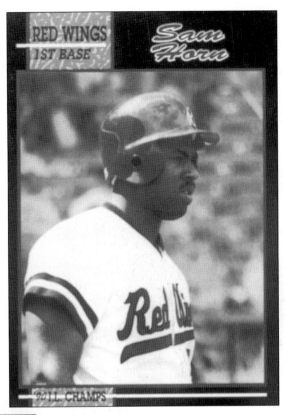

MOOSE CROSSING. Mike Mussina spent parts of two seasons with the Wings before his promotion to the big leagues, where he has starred for the Baltimore Orioles and New York Yankees. The pitcher known as "Moose" had no decisions with a 1.35 ERA in 1990. He went 10-4 with a 2.87 ERA the following season to earn International League Pitcher of the Year honors and lead the Wings to their ninth Governors' Cup.

117

"MICKEY MANTO." Jeff Manto spent only one season with the Wings, but it was a memorable one. During the summer of 1994, he clubbed 31 home runs and drove in 100 runs to earn International League MVP honors. The slugging third baseman was a big hit with the fans, spending extra time with them before and after games to sign autographs and converse. Manto, nicknamed "Mickey" after legendary slugger Mickey Mantle, was inducted into the Red Wings Hall of Fame in 2002.

MARVELOUS MARV. The second winningest manager of the Orioles affiliation, Marv Foley was a huge fan favorite. In 1997, he guided the Wings to their 10th Governors' Cup title in their first season at Frontier Field.

HOME SWEET HOME. For 68 seasons, Silver Stadium served as the home of the Rochester Red Wings.

Red Wings

50¢

1995 ROCHESTER RED WINGS SCORECARD
THE FINAL SEASON AT SILVER STADIUM

STADIUM CRUSADER. Bob Matthews, a longtime columnist for the Rochester *Times-Union* and *Democrat and Chronicle*, championed long and hard for the construction of a new ballpark to replace run-down Silver Stadium. In 1996, Matthews's tireless efforts on behalf of Rochester's sports fans were rewarded as brand-new Frontier Field opened for business.

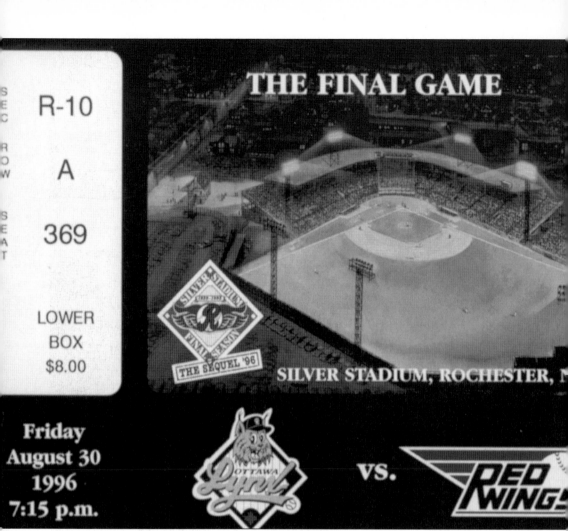

THE FINAL GAME

SEC R-10

ROW A

SEAT 369

LOWER
BOX
$8.00

Friday
August 30
1996
7:15 p.m.

SILVER STADIUM, ROCHESTER, N

VS.

SILVER SWAN SONG. On August 31, 1996, a crowd of 12,756 turned out to say goodbye to Silver Stadium. Ottawa beat Rochester 8-5 that night, but the Wings qualified for the playoffs. Their real last game at 500 Norton Street was September 10 that year, when Columbus won 4-0 in game two of the Governors' Cup finals. Only 5,573 were on hand for that game.

SPIKES'S DEBUT. On November 1, 1996, the Rochester Red Wings unveiled their new one-in-the-same logo and mascot. Spikes, a baseball-cap-wearing bird, was designed by an artist whose surname was DiMaggio. He was no relation to baseball legend Joe DiMaggio.

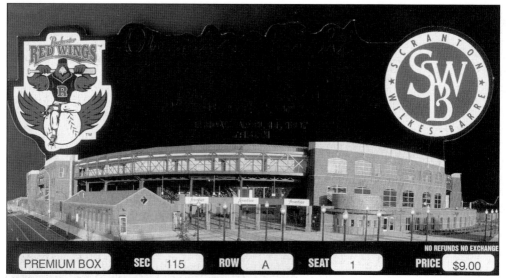

PREMIUM BOX   SEC 115   ROW A   SEAT 1   NO REFUNDS NO EXCHANGE   PRICE $9.00

1997
ROCHESTER
RED WINGS
YEARBOOK

The Inaugural Season at Frontier Field

A New Frontier. The Red Wings opened their $40 million retro ballpark in the shadow of Eastman Kodak's world headquarters on April 11, 1997. A crowd of 13,277 showed up to watch the Wings christen their ballpark with a loss to Scranton–Wilkes-Barre. Big crowds were the norm that season as the Wings set an attendance record with 540,842 tickets sold.

SAYONARA, HIDEKI. Japanese pitching sensation Hideki Irabu made his final minor-league start at Frontier Field against Rochester on June 30, 1997, before being called up by the New York Yankees. The Red Wings were not gracious hosts, roughing up Irabu for eight hits and four runs in five innings in front of an electrified crowd of 13,485.

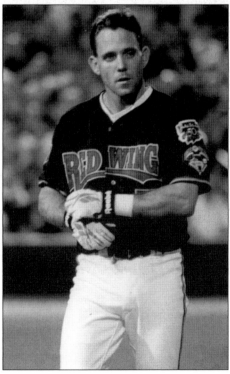

THE CATCH OF THE DAY. Perhaps the most important catch in Wings history took place in the final game of the 1997 Governors' Cup finals against the Columbus Clippers at Frontier Field. Rochester was clinging to a 4-3 lead with one out in the ninth when Homer Bush laid down a surprise bunt. Wings third baseman P.J. Forbes (pictured here) sprinted roughly 45 feet and dove head-first to make the catch. Brian Shouse then retired Matt Howard on a flyout as the Wings won their 10th Governors' Cup in their first season at Frontier.

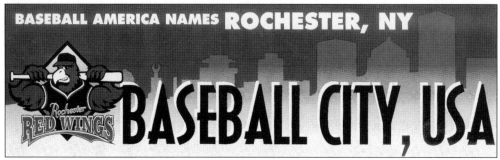

BASEBALL AMERICA NAMES ROCHESTER, NY

BASEBALL CITY, USA

Tops in Their Field. Before the turn of the century, *Baseball America* magazine proclaimed Rochester "Baseball City, U.S.A." The selection was based on a number of criteria, including fan support, history, and facilities.

A Perfect 10. Jim Wawruck lifts the Governors' Cup in celebration after the Wings defeated the Columbus Clippers in the decisive fifth game of the 1997 International League championship series. It marked the 10th time in franchise history that Rochester had won the Governors' Cup.

THE TRIUMPHANT TRIO. The three winningest managers during the Orioles era—Marv Foley, Johnny Oates, and Joe Altobelli—are pictured here at Frontier Field during the summer of 2000. Among them, they won four Governors' Cups.

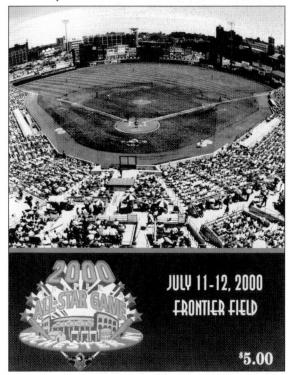

STARRY, STARRY NIGHT. Frontier Field served as the site for the Triple-A All-Star Game on July 12, 2000.

A Milestone Return. Cal Ripken Jr. was honored before the Orioles 1997 exhibition game against the Wings when banners were unfurled from the top of the Art Craft Optical building across the railroad tracks from Rochester's Frontier Field. (Courtesy of Jamie Germano.)

On the Fast Track. During the summer of 2001, Tim Redding, a former star pitcher at Churchville-Chili High School and Monroe Community College, made his major-league debut with the Houston Astros at age 23. Redding became the first born and bred Rochesterian to play in the big leagues in nearly two decades. (Courtesy of Tim Redding.)

THE WINNER'S CIRCLE. In a promotion that attracted national attention, the Wings arranged for Zippy Chippy, the losingest thoroughbred in North American history, to race against one of their players—at Frontier Field. Outfielder Jose Herrera, shown holding the trophy, triumphed in 2000, but Zippy prevailed the next two years, defeating Darnell McDonald and Larry Bigbe.

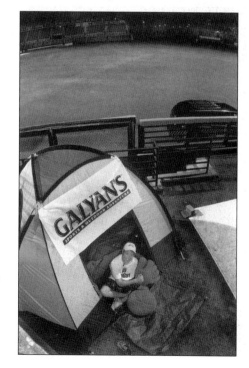

PITCHING A TENT. In an attempt to snap a late-season losing streak during the summer of 2002, Wings general manager Dan Mason slept in the home-team bullpen at Frontier Field. He endured several long nights as Rochester tied a franchise record with 12 consecutive losses.

THE BIRTH OF TWINS. In mid-September, after 42 seasons, the Wings severed ties with the Baltimore Orioles and joined forces with the Minnesota Twins. Here, Twins general manager Terry Ryan signs the player development contract as Wings president Gary Larder looks on in the visitors' clubhouse at Frontier Field. It is only the third major-league affiliation the Wings have had in their 75-year existence.